A LOOK AT MINERALS

FROM GALENA TO GOLD

Jo S. Kittinger

A First Book
Franklin Watts
A Division of Grolier Publishing
New York ■ London ■ Hong Kong
■ Sydney ■ Danbury, Connecticut

Cover and interior design by Molly Heron

Photographs ©: Art Resource: 4 (Erich Lessing), 34 (Aldo Tutino); Breck P. Kent: 37 (Smithsonian Institute), 14, 17, 18, 27, 40, 42, 50 right, 50 left, 37; Folio, Inc.: 44; Fundamental Photos: 19 (Diane Schiumo), 10, 11, 13, 21 bottom, 23, 28, 31 (Paul Silverman); GIA and Tino Hammid: 51 (Courtesy: Suzanne Tennenbaum); GIA Stone Collection: 43, 45, 39 (Robert Weldon); Lauré Communications: 49; Photo Researchers: 38 bottom (Biophoto Associates), 41 (M. Clavel), cover, back cover, 29 (Martin Land/SPL), 7 (Doug Martin), 32 (Tom McHugh), cover, back cover (Alfred Pasieka/SPL), 8 (Nuridsany et Perennou), 53 (Benelux Press), 22 (Vanessa Vick), cover, back cover (Virginia P. Weinland), cover, back cover, 36 (Charles D. Winters); Reinhard Brucker: 35; Tony Stone Images: cover, back cover (Andrew Syred), 46 (Reg Watson); Visuals Unlimited: cover, back cover, 12 (Cabisco), 25 (A.J. Copley), 21 top (Beth Davidow), 38 top (Dane S. Johnson), 6 (Doug Sokell).

Library of Congress Cataloging-in-Publication Data

Kittinger, Jo S.
A look at minerals : from galena to gold / by Jo S. Kittinger.
    p. cm. — (A First book)
Includes bibliographical references and index.
    Summary: Describes the makeup, formation, appearance,
    and uses of certain minerals, including some gemstones.
    ISBN 0–531–20385-9 (lib.bdg.)   0-531-15925-6 (pbk.)
    1. Minerals—Juvenile literature. 2. Precious stones—
Juvenile literature [1. Minerals. 2. Precious stones.] I. Title.
II. Series.
QE365.2.K57   19998
549—dc21   98-22677
                                      CIP
                                      AC

GROLIER
PUBLISHING

CONTENTS

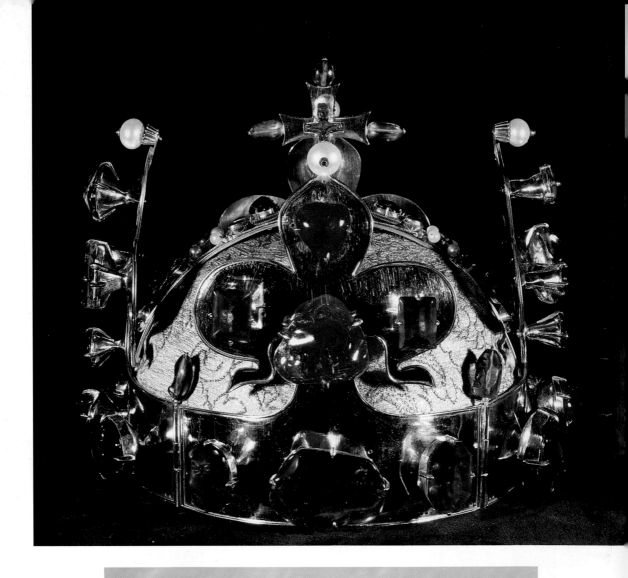

Precious minerals have symbolized wealth and power for thousands of years. This crown for the kings of Bohemia, made in the mid-1300s, is made of gold adorned with pearls and priceless gems such as sapphires (blue stones) and rubies (deep-red stones).

ONE

MAGNiFiCENT MiNERALS

WINDOWS OF jewelry stores sparkle with treasure. You pay high prices for gleaming gold and *gems*. Uncut gems and gold *ore*, however, are free to the original finder. Precious *metals* and *gemstones* make up only a small part of Earth's rich resources. Our Earth is packed with valuable *minerals* just waiting to be found.

Minerals are solid materials that naturally occur on Earth, other planets, moons, and meteorites. Different kinds of minerals combine to form rocks, though minerals can be found in other forms as well. There are approximately 3,000 different kinds of minerals on Earth, but only about a hundred are common.

Minerals combine to form rocks such as this granite. If you look carefully, you can see grains of individual minerals including quartz, mica, and feldspar. Together, the different grains give the rock its mottled appearance.

Before we can fully understand minerals, we need to know about *elements*. An element is the simplest kind of substance that can exist in the chemical world. An element cannot be broken down into simpler substances under normal circumstances. The smallest possible particle of an element is called an *atom*. An atom is so small it can only be seen with the most sophisticated microscopes.

Each kind of mineral is made up of a specific arrangement of elements. The arrangement of chemical elements in a mineral is called the chemical composition.

Some minerals, such as gold, diamond, and graphite are composed of only one element. Pure gold is composed entirely of gold atoms. Both diamond and graphite are minerals made entirely of carbon atoms, though the carbon atoms are structured very differently in each mineral. However, most minerals are *compounds*, meaning they are made up of two or more elements. Quartz is an example of a mineral that is made up of more than one element. This glassy mineral is composed of the elements silicon and oxygen.

This quartz crystal is made of a combination of the elements silicon and oxygen.

Scientists often refer to elements by one-letter or two-letter symbols. For example, the symbol for silicon is Si and the symbol for oxygen is O. Element symbols can be grouped together into formulas showing which elements make up a particular mineral. For example, the formula for quartz is SiO_2. This means that there is one atom of silicon for every two atoms of oxygen in a piece of quartz.

Minerals are *crystalline*. This means the atoms or groups of atoms are structured in a specific pattern. Liquid water is a natural, inorganic structure with a specific chemical composition (H_2O). Is it a mineral? No, water is not considered a mineral because it is not solid and it is not crystalline. Ice, on the other hand, is considered a mineral because it is solid and forms *crystals*. You probably have seen one form of ice crystals falling from the sky. We call them snowflakes.

You might say some minerals, such as turquoise and gold, look like blobs, not crystals. However, if you looked under a powerful microscope, you could see that the mass is crystalline. It is composed of tiny crystals.

Although liquid water is not a mineral, ice is a mineral because it is solid and forms crystals such as this snowflake.

Classifying Minerals

People who study minerals are called mineralogists. Mineralogists are trained to identify and classify minerals by checking five main mineral characteristics. These characteristics are *specific gravity*, *hardness*, *cleavage*, *luster*, and *streak*.

Specific gravity is a comparison of the weight of the mineral with the weight of an equal amount of water. For example, 1 cubic centimeter (0.06 cubic inches) of water weighs 1 gram (0.035 ounces). The same amount of gold, however, weighs 19.3 grams (0.68 ounces). Because gold is 19.3 times heavier than an equal amount of water, it has a specific gravity of 19.3.

The hardness of a mineral refers to its ability to withstand being scratched. German mineralogist Friedrich Mohs invented a scale comparing the hardness of various minerals. *Mohs' scale* lists ten minerals and numbers them one to ten from the softest to the hardest. The hardness of any mineral is determined by whether it can

Mohs' Scale of Mineral Hardness

Mohs' #	Mineral	Description of Hardness
1	Talc	Easily scratched with a fingernail
2	Gypsum	Easily scratched with a fingernail
3	Calcite	Easily scratched with a copper coin
4	Fluorite	Easily scratched with pocketknife
5	Apatite	Easily scratched with pocketknife
6	Feldspar	Not easily scratched with a pocketknife
7	Quartz	Cannot be scratched with a good steel file
8	Topaz	Cannot be scratched with a good steel file
9	Corundum	Cannot be scratched with a good steel file
10	Diamond	Scratches all other minerals

Higher numbers indicate harder minerals. Window glass has a hardness of about 5.5.

scratch, or be scratched by, the ten minerals on Mohs'
scale. Each mineral on the scale can be scratched by all
the minerals with higher numbers.

The softest mineral, talc, is number one. Talc can be
scratched by all the other minerals on Mohs' scale. Diamond is number ten. Only another diamond can scratch
a diamond.

The hardness of a mineral is determined partially by
the kinds of elements it contains. The way the atoms of
the elements attach (or bond) to each other, however, is
just as important in determining the hardness of a mineral. You remember that both diamond and graphite,

Although diamond (left) and graphite (right) are both
made entirely of carbon, they are very different
because the carbon atoms are arranged differently
in each mineral. Diamond is the hardest of all
minerals while graphite is very soft.

the "lead" in your pencils, are formed from carbon atoms. Yet diamond is the hardest mineral in the world while graphite is very soft. In graphite, the bonds between carbon atoms are weak. In a diamond, the carbon atoms are forced into very tight bonds under extreme pressure deep underground. This makes diamond much harder than graphite.

You might think you could test diamonds to see if they were real by hitting them with a hammer. That would be an expensive way to learn that just because a mineral is hard does not mean it will not break. Diamonds and other minerals break because of a property called cleavage.

Cleavage is the tendency of minerals to break along flat surfaces. These flat areas where the mineral breaks easily are called cleavage planes. Cleavage planes exist where the atoms or groups of atoms of a mineral are bonded together relatively weakly. Minerals cleave in different ways depending on their structure. Have you ever seen mica? It splits in one direction, form-

Mica splits into thin sheets along its cleavage plane.

11

Diamonds form pyramids when split along their cleavage planes.

ing thin sheets. Diamonds form pyramids when broken along their four cleavage planes.

Some minerals do not contain cleavage planes. These minerals break into irregular shapes. This is called *fracture*. Native Americans were able to chip quartz into arrowheads because it splinters off in smooth, curved pieces. This is called *conchoidal fracture*. If you look at broken glass, you will see that it breaks in the same way.

The luster of a mineral is a description of how the surface looks when it reflects light. Pure metals such as gold and platinum are shiny. This is called a metallic luster. Other minerals that contain metal elements also may have a metallic luster. You may have seen pyrite, a mineral that contains iron. It is sometimes called "fool's gold" because it shines like the real thing but is not precious.

Minerals that do not look metallic have a nonmetallic luster. These minerals may be waxy-looking, dull, pearly, satiny, or greasy. *Vitreous* means it looks glassy. *Adamantine*, the brightest luster, means it gleams like a diamond.

Quartz does not have any cleavage planes. The irregular, shell-shaped break on top of this smoky quartz crystal is called a conchoidal fracture.

Do not count on the color of a mineral for identification. Many minerals come in a variety of colors because of impurities in the stones. But mineralogists do check a mineral's streak. This is the color, if any, that is left when a mineral is scraped across a special unglazed tile. Often the streak is the same color as the stone. Magnetite, a

Hematite looks silvery-black, but it leaves a reddish streak.

silvery-black mineral leaves a black streak. However, sometimes the streak is quite different. Hematite, which is also silvery-black, leaves a dark, cherry-red streak.

The precious metals and fantastic gems at jewelry stores are a shining example of the treasure our Earth contains. However, many other minerals, though not as pretty, are still valuable. In a sense they are priceless, because we need them to manufacture items we use daily—everything from pottery to medicine to automobiles.

TWO

MATCHLESS METALS

Look around. How many things are made of metal? There are cars, airplanes, tools, and jewelry, to name a few. Metals are very important to our civilization. In fact, historians have divided human history into several periods based on what metals were used during each period. The Stone Age ended and the Bronze Age began around 3000 B.C. when people first learned to make tools out of bronze (a blend of copper and tin). During the following period, the Iron Age (1500 to 1000 B.C.), many people began to use iron to make stronger tools.

Metals have a metallic luster—they reflect light and look shiny. Electricity and heat flow easily through metal. Most metals are *malleable*. This means they can be hammered into thin sheets. Most metals are also *ductile*, meaning they can be pulled into thin wire. These properties make them very useful in industry.

The majority of Earth's elements are metals. However, it is rare to find any metal occurring naturally in its pure state. They combine with other elements, forming compound minerals that are not themselves metals. Minerals that contain enough metal to be mined profitably are called ores. The metals must be removed from the minerals before they can be used. *Smelting* is a process in which ore is melted to remove the metal it contains. Iron, tin, lead, and zinc are among the metals we get from ores.

Common minerals with a metallic luster include magnetite, galena, and pyrite. Magnetite is the richest ore for iron. Black magnetite crystals contain so much iron they are attracted to magnets. In fact, some magnetite, called *lodestone,* is itself magnetic. Hematite, though less rich in iron than magnetite, is the most abundant and important iron ore.

Galena is a soft, heavy, silvery-gray mineral that contains the elements lead and sulfur. Galena frequently forms rough, cube-shaped crystals. It was probably one of the earliest minerals to be smelted. Galena was thrown into fires so the lead would melt out. When the ashes cooled, the lumps of lead could be retrieved. Archaeologists have found pieces of lead around campfire sites dating back 5,000 years. During the American Civil War in

Galena forms rough, cube-shaped crystals.

the United States, Confederate and Union troops fought to control rich deposits of galena in Missouri. Whoever controlled the galena would have lead for bullets.

Pyrite, a mineral that contains iron and sulfur, forms fantastic crystals of various shapes. It can be found as jumbled cubes, eight-sided crystals called octahedrons, or flat pyrite "suns." The name pyrite comes from the Greek word *pyra,* meaning "fire." When struck with a hammer, pyrite produces sparks. Ancient Greeks believed pyrite actually contained fire that could be

Pyrite is called fool's gold because some people have mistaken it for the real thing.

knocked out when the stone was struck. Pyrite is called fool's gold because it has a brassy-yellow metallic luster. Don't let it fool you. Pyrite is much harder and more brittle (less malleable) than real gold, but not as heavy. Pyrite has a specific gravity of only 5, much lighter than 19.3 for gold. However, pyrite has a Mohs' hardness of 6.5, much harder than gold's 2.5. Pyrite leaves a greenish-black or brown-black streak; gold will leave a golden-yellow to reddish streak when scraped across a tile. Although many gold prospectors have kicked aside pyrite as worthless, pyrite is mined for industrial purposes. The sulfur in pyrite can be removed to make sulfuric acid and other products. Tiny grains of gold are often found along with pyrite.

Native Elements

A handful of metallic minerals occur as native elements. This means they occur naturally in the earth's crust in their pure forms, not mixed with other elements. You might find gold, silver, platinum, or copper as native elements.

Gold has a special attraction for people. For more than 5,000 years people have searched for it, treasured it, stolen it, and killed for it. Gold is almost impossible to destroy. It never *tarnishes* or loses its shine. Acids cannot harm it. Gold recovered from sunken ships is unaffected by the salt wa-

Gold sometimes occurs as nuggets (center). It can be hammered into very thin sheets (corners) called gold leaf.

ter. It is more ductile and malleable than any other metal. One ounce (28.35 g) of gold can be drawn into a fine golden wire more than 1 mile (1.6 kilometers) long or hammered into a thin sheet covering 100 square feet (9.3 sq meters). Gold's chemical symbol, Au, comes from *aurum*, the Latin word for gold.

Gold rises up from beneath the surface of the earth and collects in long cracks in the rock that makes up the earth's crust. These underground deposits of gold are called veins or lodes. Sometimes, over time, forces within the earth push veins of gold to the surface. Once exposed, the gold can be slowly eroded out of the surrounding rock by water, ice, sun, cold, and wind. The gold is then washed into streams where the heavy mineral settles to the bottom of the streambed. Areas where loose gold can be found at the bottom of streams are called *placer deposits*. You may have seen pictures of people trying to find gold in streambeds using pans or similar devices. This is called placer mining.

Gold is rarely found in its crystal form. More commonly it occurs as small grains or flakes. Occasionally, odd-shaped nuggets turn up. One of the largest nuggets ever found weighed about 156 pounds (70.8 kg)! Named the Welcome Stranger, it was turned up accidentally by a wagon wheel in Australia in 1869.

Silver is also rarely found as crystals. However, in Kongsberg, Norway, wire-like crystalline forms of silver can be found. Silver can be hard to spot outdoors because

Placer miners use devices such as this table washer to separate gold from dirt dug up out of a streambed. As water flows over the dirt, it washes away the soil, leaving the heavier gold behind.

A silver necklace rests on top of a rock containing veins of silver.

This diamond is set in a ring made of platinum.

it tarnishes to a dull gray-black color and is generally mixed with other minerals. In the United States, few mines are worked for their silver alone. In fact, most of the world's silver is recovered as a *by-product* of mining copper, lead, and zinc. Like gold, silver is very malleable and ductile, which makes it easy to work into decorative objects. Silver also conducts heat and electricity better than any other metal. Therefore, it is used widely in the electronics industry.

Platinum is one of the heaviest substances on earth. A cup of platinum would weigh 21 times as much as a cup of water. The name platinum comes from *platina*—Spanish for "little silver." Polished platinum looks similar to polished silver, but it is much harder and will not tarnish. This makes platinum perfect for fine jewelry.

When flakes of this silvery metal were discovered in placer deposits in Columbia, South America, in 1741, it was actually considered a nuisance. But gold miners soon figured out that platinum could be added to gold without being detected. The king of Spain was worried about the gold being polluted so he sent soldiers to shut down the platinum mining. Today, the platinum he feared is far more valuable than the gold he treasured.

Copper is one of our most useful metals. You are fa-

When copper is exposed to air, it tarnishes. This causes old pennies to be much darker than new pennies.

miliar with this metal because it is used to make pennies. Like silver, copper will tarnish. Compare a new penny to an old penny. The luster changes from bright and shiny to dull. You can restore the shine by polishing copper. Until 1982, pennies in the United States were made of 95 percent copper. Then the price of copper skyrocketed, so the government began making pennies from zinc thinly coated with copper. Only silver conducts electricity better than copper, but copper is much less expensive than silver. More than half the copper mined is used in the electrical industry. Copper wires, covered by plastic, are used to carry electricity through most homes. Cooking pans are often made of copper because it heats evenly.

THREE

THE POWER OF CRYSTALS

In a world of ordinary rocks, it is exciting to find beautiful crystals. Crystals have fascinated people throughout history. Even today, some believe crystals hold special powers. One thing is true, mineral crystals are used powerfully in our lives every day.

You most likely have halite in your kitchen. Halite is a compound of the elements sodium and chlorine. It usually forms clear crystals shaped like nearly perfect cubes. The salt you sprinkle on french fries is really hundreds of tiny halite crystals. Halite has three cleavage directions, perpendicular to each other, causing large cubes to break into tiny

A magnified salt (halite) crystal

cubes. Look at salt with a magnifying glass and you can see these.

If you have been swimming in the ocean you know salt dissolves in water. Sylvite and sal ammoniac are two other minerals that dissolve in water. Halite, sylvite, and sal ammoniac belong to a group of soft minerals called the halides.

Salt has been prized for thousands of years. Not only does salt add flavor to food, it also keeps food from spoiling. This was important before refrigerators and modern canning methods were invented. Your body needs salt to maintain a proper balance in your body's fluids, such as the blood. It is also important for nerve and muscle functions. Without salt, you might suffer muscle cramps, grow weak, and feel nauseous. However, there is so much salt in processed foods today, you get all the salt you need without ever touching a saltshaker.

Salt used to be so valuable that it was used as money in many countries. Roman soldiers were paid with salt. The word "salary" came from *salarium,* a Latin word that means salt-money. Today it is hard to imagine being paid with salt crystals. However, you probably would not argue about being paid with other crystals such as diamonds. Salt is cheap now, but at one time it was just as valuable as gold.

Sulfur, a common element, is part of many compound minerals. Pyrite, you remember, is a compound of sulfur and iron. However, sulfur also occurs as a native element, forming beautiful lemon-yellow crystals. Sulfur is lightweight, fragile, and very soft (1.5 to 2.5 on Mohs' scale). Its crystal structure is made of rings of sulfur atoms loosely bonded together. Sulfur is a very poor conductor of heat. Just the heat from your hand can cause a sulfur crystal to crack. Sulfur will burst into blue flames if thrown into a fire. Burning sulfur produces a colorless but foul-smelling gas called sulfur dioxide. When this gas mixes into clouds the result can be acid rain. Acid rain kills living things in water and on land.

Sulfur crystals

However, sulfur is also used in medicines that help people. The bulk of sulfur mined is used to make sulfuric acid, one of the world's most important commercial chemicals.

Mineral sulfur has a simple chemical formula (S) because it is a native element. Some minerals that are compounds of several elements have complex chemical formulas. The formula for staurolite, for example, is $Fe_2Al_9Si_4O_{22}(OH)_2$. This mineral forms reddish-brown to black crystals called "fairy stones." Sometimes staurolite forms two or more crystals joined together symmetri-

Twinned gypsum crystals are sometimes called swallowtails or fishtails.

cally. This type of crystal growth is called *twinning*. Staurolite has little commercial value, but people who find fairy stones like to make them into necklaces or keychains. Geologists, scientists who study rocks and minerals, find staurolite useful because it gives them clues about the history of the surrounding rock.

Twinning is also common in the clear mineral gypsum. Twinned gypsum crystals are often called swallowtail crystals because they look like a bird's tail. Although the internal structure of a mineral always stays the same, the outward crystal forms can be different. Each different crystal form is called a *habit*. In addition to twinned crystals and regular crystals, gypsum occurs as a reddish, flower-shaped group of crystals called a "desert rose." The color comes from reddish sand that is mixed with the gyp-

A desert rose in the Sahara in northern Africa

sum. Gypsum does not always take the habit of any of these crystal shapes. When gypsum does not have the freedom of space to grow visible crystals, the mineral occurs as a formless mass, called *massive* gypsum. You can't see crystals in the massive form of a mineral, but internally the mineral retains its crystalline structure. The internal crystalline structure of a massive mineral can only be seen with a microscope, if at all.

Massive gypsum is called alabaster, and it is used to carve sculptures. An alabaster likeness of the ancient pharaoh Tutankhamen was found in his tomb in Egypt. Plaster of paris, a substance frequently used to make artwork, is also made from gypsum.

Varieties of Quartz

Quartz is one of our most common minerals. As mentioned before, it is made of a compound of silicon and oxygen with the formula SiO_2. It occurs in various crystal and massive forms, and it is contained in granite, sandstone, and many other rocks. We use quartz frequently in our daily lives. Sand, which is made of quartz, is the main ingredient when making glass. Quartz is also part of the timing mechanism in many watches.

Quartz frequently occurs as beautiful crystals. The Greek word for quartz, *krystallos,* means "ice." People once believed that clear quartz crystals were made of ice that had permanently frozen. Our word "crystal" comes from this Greek word.

Pure quartz crystals, called rock crystal, are clear and colorless. Colored quartz crystals are created by impurities in the crystals or by changes in the crystal structure. Quartz stones are often used in jewelry. The most popular variety is amethyst, a purple quartz crystal that is February's birthstone.

The ancient Greeks left us this myth about how amethyst got its color. An angry Greek god, Bacchus, swore to have his tigers eat the first person he saw. He spotted a girl named Amethyst walking in the forest and had his beasts attack. The maiden called to the goddess Diana for help. Diana changed the girl into a statue to save her from being eaten. Bacchus was sorry for

Quartz comes in many forms. Sand (center) is a common form of quartz. Other varieties (clockwise from top) are rose quartz, rock crystal, picture jasper, smoky quartz, amethyst, and citrine.

Amethyst and poured wine on her stone image, staining it purple. This may have some connection to the legend that wearing amethyst will prevent you from getting drunk. The Greek word *amethystos* means "not drunk."

Other *transparent* quartz varieties include citrine, which is yellow to amber, and smoky quartz, which is smoky gray to brown. Rose quartz, a pink variety of quartz, is translucent. This means light passes through it, but it is not really see-through. There are other interesting varieties of quartz. Rutilated quartz is a transparent rock crystal that contains golden, needle-like crystals of a mineral called rutile within the quartz crystal. Tiger's eye (or cat's eye) is an *opaque* stone that, when polished, shimmers with bands of gold and brown quartz fibers. This shimmering effect is called *chatoyancy*. Sometimes the stone has a single band of light that resembles the eye of a cat. The same stone is called hawk's eye when blue.

FOUR

EARTH'S TREASURE CHEST

WHAT DO you picture when you think of crown jewels or engagement rings? Almost all fine jewelry is made of minerals. Gold, silver, or platinum settings hold cut or polished stones. Rarity, beauty, and durability are required to make a mineral valuable as a gemstone. Opal, turquoise, *garnet*, and topaz are among minerals sometimes referred to as "semi-precious" stones. These minerals are generally less valuable than "precious" gems such as diamonds, emeralds, and rubies. However, "semi-precious" and "precious" are not necessarily accurate terms. A rare black opal can be much more valuable than a poor-quality diamond.

Like quartz, opal is made of a compound of silicon and oxygen (this compound, which has the formula

The flashes of color in opal are called fire.

SiO_2, is called silica). Opal, however, is not a true mineral because it does not have a crystalline structure. It is considered a *mineraloid* because it satisfies all the other conditions of mineral classification.

Opal is also different from quartz in that it contains water. It is made of microscopic spheres of silica packed together like marbles in a fish bowl. Water fills in the small areas between the spheres. In some kinds of opal, light reflects and bounces among the silica balls and water, producing flashes of color. This is called fire or play of color. Opal with dancing rainbows is called precious opal. Opal without fire is called common opal. The more fire an opal has, the more valuable it is. Precious opal can have a clear, white, or black background. Clear, reddish-orange opals, found in Mexico, are called fire opals even though they usually have no fire. Opal, known as the "queen of gems," is a birthstone for October.

Turquoise is a beautiful sky-blue mineral. Turquoise has always been an important mineral to Native Americans, who make jewelry and other items from turquoise and silver. Legend has it that turquoise can warn you of danger or illness by changing color, but there is no scientific basis for this.

Turquoise is usually found in massive form as veins in broken rocks. Massive turquoise is very soft. Most turquoise sold in jewelry today has been treated to make it harder. Crystals of turquoise are extremely rare and are always very tiny. If your birthday is in December, turquoise is your birthstone.

Topaz is November's birthstone. It comes in a variety of colors from colorless to transparent shades of yellow, pink, brown, blue, and green. Topaz can grow into enormous crystals weighing up to 600 pounds (270 kg). Early in history, topaz was recommended to cure madness and to prevent anger. Perhaps a gift of topaz would help next time you get a bad report card. Today, however, topaz is not believed to have any medicinal value.

Garnet is the birthstone for January. Garnet is not actually just one mineral; it is a group of minerals

This Navajo Indian bracelet is made of turquoise set in silver.

Cut and uncut topaz

that have a similar structure and composition. Almandine is a bright or deep red garnet. Pyrope is dark red, orange-red, or purplish. These two species are the typical garnets found in jewelry. Grossular garnets can be green or orange. If you look at these and other species and varieties of garnets, you can find stones of almost every color except blue. Garnets 3 feet (0.9 m) across have been found at Gore Mountain in New York. Most garnets are not pretty enough for jewelry, but they are hard enough (6.5 to 7.5 on Mohs' scale) to be ground up and made into sandpaper or emery boards.

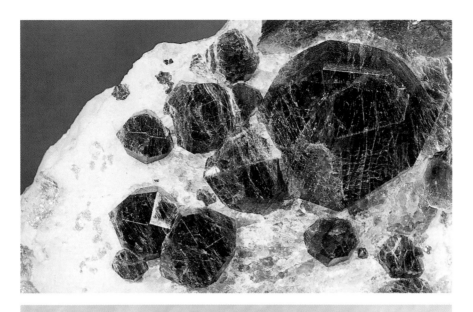

Almandine garnet crystals

The popularity and, therefore, the value of various gems has changed a great deal throughout history. Diamonds are valuable today, but they didn't become very popular until the late 1600s. Rubies, sapphires, and emeralds have been valued for much longer.

Rubies and sapphires are actually the same mineral. Both are varieties of the mineral corundum. Blood-red corundum is known as ruby. You may think that diamonds are the most expensive gem. Actually, ruby is the rarest and most valuable. Most people picture sapphires as blue, but sapphires can be many colors, including

Corundum naturally forms barrel-shaped crystals. Red corundum is called ruby.

Sapphires may not look very impressive in their rough form (right). They must be cut and polished (left) before their inner beauty shows.

pink, green, violet, gray, or yellow. All gem-quality corundum that is not red is called sapphire.

Sapphires and rubies are transparent, but sometimes you can see other materials contained within the crystal. These are called *inclusions*. Sometimes, bundles of tube-like inclusions cause a six-rayed star effect known as *asterism*. Corundum with asterism is called star ruby or star sapphire, depending on the color. Star sapphires have been called "the stone of destiny." Their three crossed lines have been said to represent faith, hope, and destiny. The "Star of India" is the largest star sapphire gem,

A star ruby

Aquamarine

weighing almost 4 ounces (113 g). You can see it and many other famous gems at the American Museum of Natural History in New York City.

Corundum, which forms barrel-shaped crystals, is very hard (9 on Mohs' scale). This hardness makes non-gem quality corundum very useful as an *abrasive* in industry.

Emerald is the name given to beautiful green crystals of a mineral called beryl. Blue or blue-green beryl is also popular for jewelry. It is called aquamarine. Though emerald and aquamarine are both beryl, emerald is much more expensive. Emerald is May's birthstone; aquamarine is one birthstone for March. Beryl also occurs in other colors. Golden beryl is yellow. Helidon is yellow and brown. Morganite is pink or red, and goshenite is clear. Individual beryl crystals can be huge. Some are longer than a school bus and weigh more than 22 small cars!

Since emerald is the most expensive variety of beryl, you might have guessed that it forms much smaller crystals. Emeralds usually contain many inclusions and *flaws*. People who make synthetic or "fake" emeralds actually put flaws in them to make them look more real.

Queen Cleopatra had emerald mines in Egypt as early as 2000 years ago. Today, beryl is mined not only for gemstones but also as a valuable ore for the rare element beryllium. Beryllium is used to make lightweight metal *alloys* for airplanes. It is also used in the nuclear industry. Materials extracted from beryl are used in fluorescent lamps and X-ray tubes.

Diamonds

Diamond, the king of gems, is the most well-known gem-

Green beryl crystals are called emeralds

41

stone. Uncut diamonds are usually eight-sided, slightly rounded crystals. The birthstone of April, diamonds form deep below the surface of the earth under intense heat and pressure in a type of blue rock called kimberlite. Sometimes, volcanic eruptions push kimberlite to the surface of the earth. Here, people may *mine* diamonds out of the kimberlite, or the crystals may be eroded naturally out of the rock. Sometimes loose diamonds settle in shallow streams or bays. In South Africa,

This diamond crystal is still embedded in kimberlite.

diamond miners actually vacuum up diamonds in shallow water off the coast.

Diamonds are graded by the four Cs: color, *clarity*, *carat*, and *cut*. Although you may think of diamonds as colorless, they can also be brown, pink, orange, violet, yellow, black, and other colors. A small amount of yellow in a diamond takes away from its value, but a richer yellow color adds to it. Desirable colors are called fancy

Diamonds are usually thought of as colorless, but they may come in several different colors. The back row of diamonds are uncut, or rough. The diamonds in the front row have been cut.

varieties. Fancy diamonds of the rarest colors—red, blue, and deep green—are the most valuable.

The most famous fancy diamond is the blue Hope Diamond. The color comes from trace amounts of boron (B) replacing carbon in the structure. The Hope Diamond has a bad reputation because many of its owners have suffered bad luck. You can see the Hope Diamond at the Smithsonian Institution in Washington, D.C. Blue diamonds are the only diamonds that can conduct electricity.

Clarity refers to how clear and how clean the stone is. Does it have undesirable inclusions or other flaws? Mineralogists and jewelers use a microscope to examine gems for internal cracks, bubbles, or anything else that disrupts the perfect clarity of the crystal. Most flaws are not visible to the naked eye.

A carat is the standard unit of weight for gemstones. One carat equals 0.2 grams (.007 ounces). A diamond and an emerald that are exactly the same size will have different carat weights because their specific gravities are different.

The large diamond in this necklace is the Hope Diamond. It is one the most famous diamonds in the world.

The largest diamond ever found was named the Cullinan. It weighed 3,106 carats, which is more than 1.3 pounds (0.6 kg). The Cullinan was cut into 105 stones, including the largest cut diamond (530 carats) now in existence—the star of Africa.

The cut of a diamond, when perfect, reflects much of the light entering the stone back up toward the viewer. This makes the diamond shine brilliantly. A well-cut di-

Various inclusions in this diamond give it poor clarity. Compare it to the much clearer diamond on page 46.

amond also breaks up light into colors of the rainbow. As with opals, the flash of colors within a diamond is called fire.

At Crater of Diamonds State Park in Murfreesboro, Arkansas, anyone can pay a small fee and look for diamonds in the blue ground—turned blue by crum-

A well-cut diamond separates light into colors of the rainbow causing it to sparkle with flashes of color.

bling kimberlite. If you are a lucky visitor, you keep any diamond you find. The largest diamond found in Arkansas, named the Uncle Sam, weighed 40.23 carats.

Only 20 percent of all diamonds mined are beautiful enough to be called gems. The remainder are used to make expensive cutting and drilling tools.

FIVE

WORK iT OUT

THE MINERALS of the earth provide priceless treasure. However, few minerals are used just as they come from the ground. Most require some changes to make them useful.

Minerals are taken out of the earth from mines. A mine is a hole or tunnel dug into the earth. Mineral deposits that lie near the surface of the earth can be removed with surface mining techniques such as quarries. Some minerals, such as diamonds, may be more than 1 mile (1.6 km) deep in the earth. These require underground mining. You might think underground mines are cool like caves, but it gets very hot in the deepest mines.

Some mines offer public tours. If you are in the Northeast, plan to visit Franklin, New Jersey,

This man is mining platinum deep within the earth in South Africa.

the "Fluorescent Mineral Capital of the World." To appreciate fluorescent minerals, you need to see them under an ultraviolet lamp. An ultraviolet lamp is called a black light because the ultraviolet light given off by the bulb is invisible. (Black lights do, however, give off a small amount of visible light as well). But fluorescent minerals absorb the ultraviolet rays and immediately begin to glow with a much brighter light. In the Sterling Hill Mine, just south of Franklin, you will be amazed when ultraviolet lamps reveal fluorescent minerals in the mine. Dull-looking rocks come alive with color under the black lights.

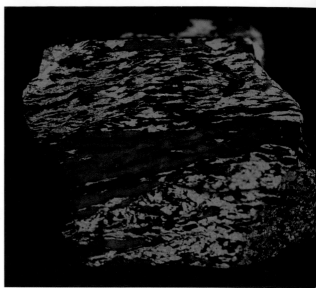

This rock from Sterling Hill Mine looks dull in regular daylight (left). But under an ultraviolet light, fluorescent minerals in the rock glow with color (right).

Small amounts of gold, silver, copper, and platinum are found as native elements. However, the vast majority of these and other metals must be removed from ores. Metals can be separated from ore by several means. Ore can be crushed, melted, or treated with chemicals to release the metals. Additional processes purify the metal.

In movies, you may have seen pirates biting gold coins. Gold is very soft (2.5 to 3 on Mohs' scale). If a coin was too hard, a pirate knew it wasn't pure gold. Often soft metals are mixed with harder metals to add strength. A mixture of two or more metals is called an alloy. Brass is an alloy of two parts of copper mixed with one part of zinc.

Gold is often alloyed with silver, copper, platinum, or nickel. Gold that naturally occurs mixed with silver is called *electrum*. The purity of gold alloys is measured in karats. One karat equals 1/24 pure gold. Thus, pure gold is 24 karat, or "24k." Eighteen-karat gold, 18k, contains 18 parts gold mixed with 6 parts of another metal. On most gold jewelry, you can find the purity in karats stamped in an inconspicuous place, such as the inside of a ring. Do not confuse karats with carats. The purity of gold is measured in karats. The weight of a gemstone is measured in carats.

This gold jewelry clasp is stamped with the name of the manufacturer and the purity of the gold. The "18k" indicates that the gold is three-quarters pure.

Metal can be worked in several ways. It can be molded, beaten, or *extruded* into the desired shape. To extrude means to force out. Metal is shaped into bars and tubes by forcing it through an opening, like toothpaste coming out of a tube. Heating metal makes it easier to work. You may have seen a blacksmith beating a piece of metal into a horseshoe. First he heats the metal in a fire. This softens the metal so it bends more easily. Metal melts when it gets very hot. Molten metal can be poured into molds to make everything from candlesticks to high school rings.

Gemstones have to be separated from the surrounding rock when they are mined. The rock that a crystal is naturally embedded in is called the *matrix*. Gemstones must then be sorted by size and quality. It takes a trained eye to determine the quality of *rough* stones. Gemstones must be cut and polished before their true beauty shows.

Cutting Gems

A person who cuts and polishes gemstones is called a *lapidary.* There are two basic types of finished stones—*faceted* stones and *cabochons.*

A cabochon is a stone cut with a flat bottom and a rounded, polished top. Just picture a marble cut in half. Opaque stones (such as opals and turquoise) and star sapphires are generally made into round or oval cabochons. Hearts and tear-drops are other popular cabochon shapes.

Transparent gemstones are usually faceted. If you look at a diamond in a ring, you will see many flat surfaces around the stone. Each flat surface is called a facet. Facets improve the reflection of light. Faceted gems come in many shapes—round, square, pear, heart, and marquis are common. The typical round diamond cut has one large facet on top, called the table, and many other facets above and below the *girdle*. The girdle is the widest section of the gem where the top and bottom come together.

Lapidaries study each stone before they begin work. They must determine where the planes of cleavage lie. A diamond will split in two if struck cleanly along a cleavage plane. However, one false strike and the diamond may cleave in an unintended direction. The lapidary also wants to remove as many flaws as he can while keeping as much of the weight of the stone as possible. After faceting, a final polish allows the light to sparkle in the stone.

You don't have to be a professional lapidary to polish stones. Rock tumblers are available through hobby shops. Tumblers remove rough edges in the same way pebbles in a stream become smooth as they tumble against each other. You add finer and finer particles of abrasive grit to your revolving tumbler over time. These small, hard grains smooth the stones. Finally, you add a polishing material to the tumbler, which gives the rocks a bright shine. Polished minerals are fun to collect and can be used to make your own jewelry.

From metal bumpers on trucks and fine gold wires in computer hardware to glass bottles and salt on pretzels, minerals touch our lives every day. In addition to supplying our basic needs, minerals give us the riches we have treasured throughout history. Precious metals and gems have adorned crowns and swords. They have filled pirate chests and all our dreams. The earth holds all these riches in the form of minerals.

Glossary

Abrasive—a material used for grinding, sanding, or polishing, such as sandpaper.

Adamantine having a bright, diamond-like luster.

Alloy a mixture of two or more metals, or a mixture of a metal with another substance.

Asterism the appearance of a star (with 4, 6, or 12 rays) in a polished mineral, caused by the play of light within the stone.

Atom the smallest particle of an element.

By-product anything produced or extracted in the process of making or mining something else.

Cabochon a gem cut so that the stone has a smooth rounded top and no facets.

Carat the unit of weight for gems. One carat equals 0.2 grams (0.007 ounces), or 200 milligrams.

Chatoyancy a "cat's eye" effect in some polished stones; a thin, bright line of reflected light across the surface.

Clarity a measure of how clear and free of flaws a gemstone is.

Cleavage the property of some minerals to break along weak, flat planes in their crystal structure.

Compound a substance made up of two or more elements chemically bonded together.

Conchoidal fracture   a type of breaking that leaves curved surfaces like the inside of a shell.

Crystal   a naturally angular shape; a solid form in which the atoms or groups of atoms are arranged in an ordered pattern that generally produces a shape with flat surfaces called facets.

Crystalline   containing atoms or groups of atoms in an ordered pattern; crystal-forming

Cut   the shape in which a gem is finished (common cuts include round, marquis, pear, heart, and emerald).

Ductile   can be stretched or drawn into a thin wire without breaking.

Electrum   a naturally occurring mixture of gold and silver.

Element   a substance that cannot be separated into different substances by ordinary chemical means. Every solid, liquid, and gas is made of elements.

Extrude   to force a metal, or other substance, through a hole to give it a certain shape.

Facet   *noun*: one of the small, flat, polished surfaces on a cut gem. *verb:* to cut or grind facets on a gemstone.

Flaw   a crack, bubble, inclusion, or other defect in a crystal.

Fracture   to break unevenly, usually a characteristic of a mineral without cleavage.

Garnet   a complex group of similar minerals: includes pyrope, almandine, grossular, andradite, spessartine, and uvarovite.

Gem   a beautiful, rare, and durable mineral that has been cut and polished for use as a jewel.

Gemstone   any mineral that can be cut and polished to make gems.

Girdle   the widest section of a faceted stone. The top and bottom facets come together at the girdle.

Habit   the general shape of a crystal. The habit gives some clues as to the conditions under which the crystal formed.

Hardness   the resistance of a mineral to being scratched. Mohs' scale provides an estimate of hardness as compared to other minerals.

inclusion   a solid substance, a liquid, or a gas trapped inside a mineral.

Lapidary   a person skilled in the cutting, polishing, and engraving of stones.

Lodestone   a magnetic peice of magnetite.

Luster   the way the surface of a stone looks when it reflects light.

Malleable   can be beaten or pressed into various shapes without breaking.

Massive   a form of a mineral that shows no visible signs (such as external flat surfaces) of its internal crystalline structure.

Matrix   the surrounding rock in which a crystal is found.

Metal   a chemical element or compound that is ductile, malleable, reflects light, and conducts heat and electricity.

Mine   *noun*: a hole or tunnel made in the earth to remove metallic ores, gemstones, minerals, or other rocks. *verb*: to remove such materials from the earth.

Mineral   elements or compounds that occur naturally and have a crystalline structure. All minerals have a definate composition that can be expressed in a chemical formula.

Mineraloid a substance that satisfies most, but not all, of the conditions of mineral classification (usually is not crystalline).

Mohs' scale a list of ten minerals, ranging from the softest to the hardest and numbered from one to ten. Used to rate the hardness of all minerals.

Opaque allows no light through; not transparent or translucent.

Ore a natural combination of elements containing enough metal to be mined for a profit.

Placer deposit a concentration of sand and gravel containing heavy minerals eroded from their original location and deposited by the action of water or glaciers.

Rough in the natural condition, not cut or polished.

Smelting the process of melting a rock or mineral in order to extract or purify metal.

Specific gravity the weight of a mineral as compared to the weight of an equal volume of water.

Streak the color, if any, left when a mineral is scraped across a special unglazed tile.

Tarnish to gradually become dull or discolored when exposed to air. The original shine and color can usually be restored with polishing.

Transparent clear; allows light to pass through so that you can see through it.

Twinning two or more crystals of the same mineral growing together in a symmetrical way.

Vitreous having a glassy luster.

58

For More information

Books

Bains, Rae. *Rocks and Minerals*. Mahwah, New Jersey: Troll Associates, 1985.

Fuller, Sue. *Rocks and Minerals*. New York: Dorling Kindersley, 1995.

Holden, Martin. *The Encyclopedia of Gemstones and Minerals*. New York: Facts on File, 1991.

McConnell, Anita. *The World Beneath Us*. New York: Facts On File, 1985.

Moody, Richard. *The Concise Illustrated Book of Rocks and Minerals*. New York: W. H. Smith Publishers, 1990.

Schumann, Walter. *Handbook of Rocks, Minerals, and Gemstones*. Boston: Houghton Mifflin, 1993.

Silver, Donald M. *Earth: The Ever-Changing Planet*. New York: Random House, 1989.

Internet Resources

Bob's Rock Shop
http://www.rockhounds.com/
This noncommercial site features more than 150 images of minerals. It also provides numerous articles on rock and mineral collecting and a list of links to other sites.

Crater of Diamonds State Park
http://www.gorp.com/gorp/location/ar/parks/crat er.htm
The official Web site for this state park near Murfreesboro, Arkansas. Any diamonds you find at the park are yours to keep!

Earthly Treasure—A Kid's Guide to the Smithsonian
http://www.si.edu/resource/tours/kidsguide/ nmnh/58.htm
Information about the Smithsonian's exhibit on minerals and gems.

Geologylink
http://www.geologylink.com
This site offers fascinating geological information geared toward students, teachers, and enthusiasts. They feature several sections dedicated to kids

Hope Diamond Information from the Smithsonian
http://160.111.7.240/resource/faq/nmnh/hope.htm
A fascinating history of one of the world's most famous diamonds.

The Image Mineral Gallery

http://www.theimage.com/mineral/minerals1.html

Photographs and descriptions of more than 80 varieties of minerals.

The Image Gemstone Gallery

http://www.theimage.com/gemstone/ gemstone.html

Photographs and descriptions of more than 20 varieties of gemstones.

The Mineral and Gemstone Kingdom

http://www.minerals.net/home.htm

Detailed information about many different minerals, sorted by hardness, popularity, color, chemical group, or other criteria.

Rockhounds Information Page

http://www.rahul.net/infodyn/rockhounds

This site includes a list of answers to questions frequently asked by rockhounds (rock and mineral collectors). They also feature a library of images, articles, and links to many other sites.

Smithsonian Gem & Mineral Collection

http://galaxy.einet.net/images/gems/ gems-icons.html

index

Italicized page numbers indicate illustrations.

About the Author

Jo S. Kittinger finds creativity in nature. As a potter, freelance crafts designer, writer, and illustrator, she can take common clay and turn it into a vase, or a summer's breeze and turn it into a story. Her work has appeared in numerous books, magazines, and newspapers. She is the author of Watts First Books *A Look at Rocks: From Coal to Kimberlite* and *Dead Log Alive!* She lives with her family and a menagerie of pets in Hoover, Alabama.